Without Ruin:

Pearls of Wisdom

for the Triumphant Woman

By: Berthena Jackson

Table of Contents

Acknowledgement

"Every good and perfect gift is from above, coming down from the Father of the heavenly lights, who does not change like shifting shadows (James 1:17, NIV).

First giving thanks to Jesus Christ, Lord of my life, and Lover of my soul. Without You where would I be? It was because of your grace and mercy that I was able to endure the hardships of my divorce. You forgave my disobedience, put my sin out of sight and cleared my record of guilt and replaced it with true happiness. When I decided to put my faith and trust in You, you set me free from fear, protected my family and I, showed me goodness, supplied my needs, listened when I called and redeemed me from a hurtful past. Thank you for trusting me with Your vision for this book. I love You and I will forever praise your Holy Name.

Thank you to my beautiful daughter Tashiana. You are a precious and beautiful gift from God. There were times I called you on the phone to encourage you because that is what mother's do; yet you surprised me with your words of wisdom. You will never know how much it meant to hear you say: "Mom, do not give up writing your book. You can do it." Those words blessed my heart. God has matured you into an intelligent woman. You bring laughter and joy to my day. I love you more than words can say.

To my handsome son Richard Alan Jr., you inspire me to take a deep breath and exhale. Your perspective on life is refreshing. You have always told me to relax, calm down; life is not that serious, and everything will work out. Thank you for reminding me that God is in control and nothing is impossible with Him. You are incredible and wise beyond your years. I am so proud of the young man you have become. Love you dearly.

Momma, thank you for raising me to think for myself and make my own decisions. You are not just my mother, you are my friend and confidante. I can share my hurt, my pain, my joy and my dreams with you without feeling judged. Thank you for your love and support during this journey. I could not have asked for a more compassionate and genuine parent. I love you always.

To my spiritual mentor, Evangelist Celie Anazoda, founder of Daughter of Zion Ministry, you are an amazing woman of God. Words cannot express my appreciation for your encouraging words of wisdom and faith. Thank you for leading me to discover my purpose. It was your, purpose driven leadership that pushed me to finish the book. You rallied behind me with the Word of God coupled with your passionate spiritual energy and drive. I remember well the words you spoke to me: "Finish the book; it will be a spiritual weapon for women". The Lord bless you and keep you; the Lord make his face to shine on you and be gracious to you. Love and blessings.

I would be remiss if I did not thank all my Spiritual Sisters: Chaconia Agywenkwah, Kamesa ONeal, Carmella Canada, Melinda Church, Tammara Oates, Melony Crawford, Joycelyn (Joy) Benneth-Shikmut and Tanya Taylor. Thank you for helping me figure out the title and the book cover image. Thank you for using your skills in photography. Thank you for your uplifting words during this writing journey: You are a fabulous support system filled with mutual love, encouragement, support, motivation, compassion and faith. You inspired me in different ways to complete this project. I

am extremely grateful for our sisterhood. May God meet all of
your needs according to the riches of his glory in Christ Jesus.
I love you all.

Prologue

Divorce is synonymous with dying, because there is a great sense of loss, separation and extreme sadness. The forces of divorce itself, add rejection and deep emotional pain to the mix. In some ways, it is more difficult to endure, and it takes additional time to heal. Much like the oyster, we want the irritant to go away, so we try everything under the sun to ease the trouble; to prevent death. Beloved you are a pearl. You are symbolic of the presence and power of God.

The pearl is valuable and worth mentioning because, it is formed after going through an arduous process. It all begins when a tiny sandstone finds its way between the oyster's mantle and shell. As a defense mechanism the oyster will quickly begin covering the uninvited intruder with layers of nacre; mother of pearl known to be a durable, resilient material that protects the oyster's vital organs. Eventually, after the continuous release of nacre, the sandstone is transformed into a beautiful, shiny pearl. The effort the oyster goes through to remove the stone, which has the capacity to cause death, reminds me of how women handle divorce. Women just want the pain to dissolve to protect their vital organ; the heart.

Persevere like the oyster. Let God cover you in His special nacre to restore and protect your heart. You do not have to stay stuck on past hurt. God affirmed his unwavering love towards you, while you were questioning if He still cared. He deemed you precious in His sight. His greatest desire was to see you healed and restored. Renewal and restoration belong to you; now, it is finished. God will make it his personal obligation to return you, unscathed to the purpose driven woman you were destined to be before the divorce.

You pushed through and gained the victory. It took time to develop your character and the Fruit of the Spirit. Break- through has finally come, and you are now more centered. You represent honor, courage and commitment; you are a beautiful pearl, replete with wisdom. A unique entity shaped by your suffering and pain. You are certainly priceless and precious in the sight of a Sovereign, all knowing and all powerful God. It was He who called you forth, out of the vicissitudes of a broken heart. Beloved sister, it is time to rise to your respectful place. He has transformed you into a resilient woman without ruin. Behold the former things have passed away and God has declared new things shall spring forth. By His infinite grace and mercy, you are a pearl.

Rock Bottom

God designed marriage to meet our need for companionship and to provide an illustration of our relationship with Him

Since I was a little girl, I dreamt of having a marriage that would last a lifetime. Not once did I weigh the seriousness of my licentious actions, until I found myself at the lowest point of life, recovering from a painful divorce. After the divorce was final, the enemy deployed to keep me in the throes of perpetual brokenness, internal torment and shame. I never imagined I would hit rock bottom. So much so that I felt disconnected from my true identity in Christ, my purpose and my destiny in the earth.

My mother never advised me to wait for marriage before having illicit sex. As young as nine years old, I watched my mother and my aunts living with men to whom they were not married. Back in my day, they called it "shacking up". A more definitive definition is to sleep or live together as unmarried sexual partners. It was definitely not the godly way to begin a relationship. At the time, I did not think my behavior was wrong. A door to sexual sin was open by way of childhood games, exposure to pornography and generational iniquity.

Given my history, it is no wonder that our engagement was preceded by sexual attraction, to the point it became impossible to remain apart. The electricity between us felt like love, so we did the next best thing and decided to marry. Yes, we were both attending church; trying our best to do what the Bible said, but our desires were more important. You discover later that a relationship built upon sexual attraction does not stand the test of time. When sexual sin is at work within our soul, our perspective concerning ourselves and God becomes deeply skewed and blurs our awareness of right and wrong.

As I unpacked the historical events leading up to my divorce, I discovered a profound truth. Satan was involved the entire time. He did not sabotage my marriage on my honeymoon or in the early years of figuring out married life. Instead, Satan began the methodical and diabolical work to destroy my marriage long before my boyfriend and I stood at the altar to recite our marriage vows. Once I accepted the wedding ring, my marriage was a target. Satan despised my marriage. I believe he watched and observed; then he began planning the destruction of my union.

Our dating and short engagement was marked with sexual impurity. What followed was a pattern of obeying my own desires instead of God's direction. It was a clever ploy; I naively fell for because no one advised me to keep my clothes on. I did not know that a woman who respects her body and keeps her clothes on is to be honored. Unfortunately, we are living in a generation where moral values have been discarded. Women are selfishly pursuing their own sexual pleasure. Young women are not being taught as soon as they have the maturity to understand, that a virtuous woman is a woman of good character and one who is highly esteemed. She is an individual who brings honor to her family because she is submitted and committed to God. She is a woman who keeps herself up to maintain her attractiveness and her skirt pulled down. She fears God.

Sexual sin starts in the heart. The Bible says: *"Out of the heart proceed evil thoughts, murders, adulteries, fornications, thefts, false witness, blasphemies" (Matthew 15:19).*

It is so easy to become tempted or drawn away by one's own desires when you are uninformed. Ignorance overshadows our understanding of how much God hates lewdness. It is an affront to God; encouraging direct and open violation of God's law. Paul was on target when he penned the following:

"They are darkened in their understanding and separated from the life of God because of the ignorance that is in them due to the hardening of their hearts. Having lost all sensitivity, they have given themselves over to sensuality so as to indulge in every kind of impurity, and they are full of greed" (Ephesian 4:18-22).

"Therefore, God over in the sinful desires of their hearts to sexual impurity for the degrading of their bodies with one another. They exchanged the truth about God for a lie and worshipped and served created things rather than the Creator – who is forever praised. Amen. Furthermore, just as they did not think it worthwhile to retain the knowledge of God, so God gave them over to a depraved mind, so that they do what ought to be done" (Romans 1:24-25, 28).

Detoxification is hard. Try as I might to detox him out of my system, I failed more times than I can count. The urge to have sex with my boyfriend during our post-dating period was strong. I could not fault him. He did not force me to get naked before him. It was a voluntary act. It was my dirty, sinful deeds that later led me to marry someone I spiritually had nothing in common with. Why did I let my guard down and get trapped in a cycle of sexual impurity? I lacked wise judgment. Deception and ignorance hid the reality of an inconspicuous killer that was already at work deep within my soul. *"Can a man scoop fire into his lap without his clothes being burned?" (Proverbs 6:27).* The answer is unquestionably, no.

The weakness of our flesh is very powerful; it fights to be in control of our actions. It opposes the Bible's teaching on holiness and purity. I was hooked on this man like an addict is hooked on drugs. When I looked in the mirror at the face staring back at me, I compared my life to the life of Nola Darling in the movie "She's Gotta Have It." Are you familiar with her story? The movie was a production created by Spike Lee in 1986. It is a portrayal of a beautiful and talented Brooklyn-based artist named Nola Darling. She struggled to stay true to herself and her dreams, while dividing her time between her friends, her job and all three of her lovers. That trio included a married businessman and father, a photographer and self-described "biracial Adonis" and a talkative, Michael Jordan fan. Like Darla, I engaged in compulsive sexual activity despite negative consequences.

Weekends could not come fast enough. All day my mind was constantly thinking about spending time with him. When my day at work ended, I hurriedly tidied up my desk, grabbed my military purse and beret, then I rushed home to pack an overnight bag. I was pressed to fill an empty void in my life that only God could fulfill.

When you are deep in sexual sin, you are consistently and persistently bombarded with thoughts that range from mildly distracting to disturbingly dark. The flesh wants you to give in to your sinful cravings and compulsions. When we should be sleeping or praying, our flesh finds the television, or answers a telephone call. When we should be diligently watching and praying our flesh wants to sleep. When we should be reading and meditating on bible scriptures, our flesh becomes distracted with creative sexual fantasy. It is so maddening!

Sexual impurity is addictive. It begins with a spark and left unchecked turns into a wildfire; devouring everything in its path. It destroys the mind, body and soul. It will singe your moral conscious unless you take definitive steps to avoid its death grip. Start by guarding your mind. Do not read books or look at pictures that encourage fantasies, which stimulate the wrong desires. Keep away from settings and friends that tempt you to sin. Focus on the future consequences of sexual sin – pregnancy, disease, inability to fulfill commitments, incapacity to feel sexual desire and failure to be transparent.

Do not make the mistake I did, my weak mind opened me up to spirits of lust, loneliness, and rejection. As I stood face to face with shame, disappointment, self-criticism and the absence of spiritual judgement, I became depressed. I was alive physically, but I was dying spiritually because I had separated from God's Lordship. One evening, as I sat in my living room wallowing in self-disgust and beating myself up for the mess I was in, I had an encounter with God. I was so downtrodden that I almost missed the renewal waiting for me at the end of a long wilderness experience, until I called on the Name of Jesus to help me break free from sexual sin. Whoever calls on the Name of Jesus will be save.

He saw my disgraced condition, yet He deemed me precious in His sight. His deepest desire was to see me healed and my relationship with Him restored. I thought I was to damaged, that renewal and restoration would never find me in the wilderness. When I remembered what Jesus had done for me in the past, I experienced unspeakable joy. He lifted me out of the slimy pit, out of the mud and mire, set my feet on solid ground and gave me a firm place to stand. I felt the warmth of God's love surround me. I was empowered to change. I was determined to push my way through the self-defeating thoughts and self-condemnation. I made a conscious decision to let the Holy Spirit take control of my life.

The moment I decided to follow Jesus and doggedly resist sexual temptation, is the moment I began the process of dying to my flesh and upgrading to a holy standard of living.

Ignorance or Accountability

Are we at fault when we are not aware of certain principles? Should a lack of knowledge really be a viable excuse? Not being aware does not mean it is unobtainable, it requires work. Ignorance distorts biblical truth and leads to sin. Ignorance does not mean you are stupid; it means you are uninformed. Oftentimes, inexperience is the root of women connecting with the wrong type of men. Engaging with a man who lacks spiritual integrity typically leads one to compromise their values.

Holiness demands adherence to strict rules regarding pure worship and wholesome conduct in mind, body and spirit. Moreover, it requires a complete commitment of will to follow the Lord's commandments. Marriages fail, or people get divorced, because their expectations were too high or unrealistic. When expectations go unmet, it leads to conflict and then breakup. No one wants to admit to their spouse that their unspoken, unreasonable and unmet expectations ruined the marriage.

Marriages fail due to incompatibility. People forget that marriage is not just about physical compatibility. Couples should be spiritually compatible and in tune with each other's feelings. Marriages fail because couples have low tolerance and they do not want to compromise. Couples with low tolerance and uncompromising attitudes are selfish. Look at old re-runs of the television show *"Divorce Court"*. If you listen carefully to why couples are in divorce court, similarities emerge. You will notice many couples on the show exhibit very low levels of tolerance and lack maturity in their outlook. When one person wants his or her way and are not flexible, they find themselves in front of the family court judge. Marriages fail due to family pressure. There are many untold stories of sons and daughters being coerced, blackmailed or shamed into a marriage not sanctioned by God. Biological mothers and fathers, and spiritual leaders such as pastors, spiritual godparents and mentors; while their heart is in the right place; they are guilty of persuading a man or woman to wed. Marriages fail due to infidelity. It is by far the number one offender. Cheating is a serious global epidemic that destroys marriages. No other transgression has the power to destroy the respect, love and trust between couples than adultery. Many temptations entice husbands and wives to leave when marriage becomes dull, in order to find excitement and pleasures elsewhere. God never intended marriage to be boring, lifeless or dull. Rather, His expectation was for couples to trust Him with their marriage. Yet couples waste God's best for them by believing the illusion, there is greener pastures somewhere else.

I was a new believer in Christ when I met my boyfriend and unfamiliar with biblical truth. The Lord was still changing the old sinful Berthena into a new creature, despite the fact of indulging my flesh. What was clearly wrong became the norm. Familiarity with sin only invites deception within one's mind and spirit. Being in perfect fellowship with God, should have helped me in my struggle with sex. We must accept His outstretched hand.

The problem with receiving God's help is that the enemy does not want you to get the help you need. He is always planting thoughts in your mind, which seem harmless, but are really hazardous to your spiritual well-being. His goal is to get you to believe the lie that purity has certain limits. He is so cunning, that he will have you believe that if you do not cross certain boundaries with your thoughts, words and deeds, you are still pristine. Purity is not overstepping the boundaries; rather it is a posture of the heart. A pure heart sees beyond the intellect and yearns for a cleaner inner life that is reflected on the outside.

It took me years, to fully comprehend the impact of my actions. My misconduct impeded God's original design for marriage. God's ways are always best, but I allowed Satan to trick me into believing my way was better than God's way. My desire to be loved was so strong, that it caused me to miss the warning signs. I convinced myself it was acceptable to have sex before marriage. Ignorantly, I believed once I was married, my unlawful sexual sin would not cost me anything. What an erroneous assumption. Sexual sin is one of the enemy's most effective strategies to corrupt the holy union of marriage before couples take their vows before God. The adversary aggressively uses persuasion to get us into a habit of resisting the spirit in that we consistently follow our sinful desires.

Many nights I wept bitterly at the unfairness of my situation. God, why? Why did you let me go through this? Why did you not send a prophet to warn me? Lord, I thought you loved me. Was I settling for a man, because I did not want to be alone? Was I settling, because I did not feel I deserved better? Had I convinced myself that a warm body lying next to me in bed was enough? I did not have the answers back then.

Years later, I learned that ignorance is bliss, because what you do not know, you do not worry about it. Ignorance gives you the freedom to keep doing what you are doing even if it is wrong. I learned that no one purposely decides to settle. No one says, "Okay, I'm going to settle with this man I am with, because I do not believe I can get what I really want." I saw my own ignorance as blind optimism, because my tendency was to focus on the positive aspects of my situation, while virtually blind to any potential pitfalls. I learned that while it is true that ignorance can be a common experience for

all people, there is real hope in Jesus Christ. If you ask God
for discernment, you can begin to understand why He allowed
something to happen. You can also discover how God can
redeem the situation and bring benefits to your life, as a result
of suffering. Though you make ignorant decisions, by the
grace of God and by the power of the Holy Spirit, you may
stand up again.

DRAGGED Away

Fish are enticed by the bait on a fishing line; it is irresistible. When the fish sees that juicy wiggling worm, it is enticed to go grab hold of it. The only problem is that once it is hooked, it can be dragged away. The fish is not always dragged away; it may get lucky and escape. The same holds true for us. When we encounter temptation, we can immediately reject it as Joseph did when Potiphar's wife tempted him.

Joseph went into his supervisor's house to perform his duties as a responsible employee, never expecting to be accosted by his boss' wife. Rumor has it, she was a seductive man-eater; waiting and watching for a foolish man to fall prey to her cunning seduction. I believe Joseph was on her radar for a while. From what I imagine, Joseph was not an unattractive man. He was young, strong, muscular and handsome. She was an experienced seductress and adulterer. A lioness waiting to devour her prey. What she did not bank on was a god-fearing man who followed the Law of God. Joseph knew better than to disrespect his boss by sleeping with his wife.

"My son keep my words and store up my commands within you. Keep my commands and you will live; guard my teachings as the apple of your eye. Bind them on your fingers; write them on the tablet of your heart. Say to wisdom, You are my sister, and to insight, You are my relative. They will keep you from the adulterous woman, from the wayward woman with her seductive words" (Proverbs 7:1-5).

Potiphar's wife thought she could use the same tactics on Joseph that she had used on other men. I envision her aggressively catching him by his cloak and attempting to persuade him with words dripping with honey to follow her to the bedroom. However, Joseph revered God more than his flesh, and that brother ran out of that house so fast, he left her standing with his cloak in her hand *(Genesis 39:11-12)*. Joseph passed the sex addiction test.

It is up to us to make the choice to yield or run. Being tempted is not sinful. It becomes sin when the evil desire drags us away from where our hearts should be. Strong desire can be either good or bad, depending upon the object of that desire and the motive behind it. When God created us, he created us with a human heart and a passionate desire to long after Him and His righteousness *(Psalm 42:1-2)*. We can make a conscious decision to go after God or our fleshly desires. As the deer pants for water, our soul should thirst for God; but more often than not, we do not thirst after our Creator.

In 2003, I was dragged away when I gave in to my lustful and unrestrained desires. My ex-husband's charisma was powerful; making it a challenge to resist temptation. Jesus said he would give me a way out of temptation, but I said no because it felt good. The chemistry between him and I was very evident. Every time I was with him, I compromised. I had no control over my feelings and emotions.

He was absolutely wonderful to hang out with. I thought he was very charming and funny. He cooked, cleaned, and did his own laundry. He was always well dressed, well-groomed and wore the best smelling cologne. He was everything I thought I wanted in a husband. Generally speaking, he had a captivating personality. However, yielding to physical feelings and emotions is never a smart idea. Your judgment vacillates, and your thoughts and your decisions become illogical.

I was dragged away by sexual temptation, because I was enticed by his good looks. God should have been the recipient of my desire. I should have been longing for a more intimate relationship with Jesus, *(Psalm 42:1-2; 73:25)* rather than the forbidden fruit that appealed to my flesh but was poison to my spirit. The devil knows what you like in a mate and he sends his best representative. I took the bait and compromised. Abstinence went out the window. Relying on my judgment, I was certain I had found a love so raw, so deep and so genuine that I would never love anyone the way I loved him. In truth, I found a man who crushed my heart with his thoughtless and unkind treatment.

After we married, he changed. He was emotionally detached, requiring constant and excessive admiration. He expected to be recognized as superior even without achievements to warrant it. Not overlooking how he exaggerated his achievements and talents; turns out these were characteristics of a narcissistic person. When you are not following God's guidelines for marriage, you do not see a man's true character. In my experience, it is conceivable to be drawn to the wrong man for all the wrong reasons.

During a brief period of solitude and self-actualization, God showed me how I agreed to marry the wrong man. In times of doubt, I followed my own advice. It is imperative for us to give ourselves to God and seek His guidance. *"Trust in the Lord with all your heart and lean not on your own understanding; in all your ways submit to him, and he will make your paths straight" (Proverbs 3:5-6).* The scripture implies that if we decide not to trust the Lord with our whole heart, and we choose to lean on our own understanding, then we will surely go in the wrong direction.

The most powerful weapon against sexual impurity is repentance. When we humble ourselves and confess our sins, He is just to forgive. Disobedience and lack of close fellowship with God, leads to marrying someone whom He did not desire you or me to marry. Be encouraged. Even in the worst instance of us choosing someone whom we should not have married, God is sovereign and in control. He can turn any situation around so we still benefit.

SoulMATE Fallacy

A book titled "Men are from Mars, Women are from Venus", by John Gray, asserts that men and women communicate well when they appreciate their differences. The story is told of a Martian man meeting the Venusian woman; the soulmate connection based on shared mutual respect and acceptance.

A soulmate is defined as a connection of minds, mutual respect, an unconditional love and total understanding. At the moment, I am convinced Martian and Venusian psychology is no longer true. Groups of people say you can have a soul friend, soul teacher, or soul mate. These are individuals you click and vibe with; sharing similar tastes, interests and passions. This person is almost a mirror image of you and push you to become a better you.

In my opinion, if you believe in the notion of soulmates, then you are less likely to work through problems, because a soulmate is supposed to be perfect. As I studied the words "soul mate" further, I began to think about Adam and Eve. They were a perfect match, the perfect spiritual couple. Two peas in a pod with common interests, Adam knew Eve. I imagine before sin entered the Garden of Eden, arguments and misunderstandings did not occur at all. The first man and woman did not need a marriage counselor. Adam and Eve was the prototype of a perfect spiritual couple. Their union was a perfect depiction of what a healthy, resilient, loving spiritual relationship should look like.

The reason we believe we have not married our divine husband, is that we were sold on the "soulmate" theory. The soulmate theory is deceptive and not a Christina idea. An ancient Greek philosopher, Plato, taught that men and women were made in one body, but separated by gods. It suggests every man and woman search the earth for their perfect spouse, so the two can again become one. Phrases like "my other half" or "my better half" actually come from this Greek myth. The problem I have with this theory is that it gives the perception that we are half persons. If women believe this lie, they will always be constantly looking for the man who will complete them and will never be their own person. Even worse, she cannot live for Christ.

Is the concept of a soulmate biblical? I do not believe so; it is merely religious dogma. The common idea of a "soulmate" is that for every person, there is another person who is a "perfect fit," and if you marry anyone other than this soul mate, you will never be happy. The soulmate concept is often used as an excuse for divorce. People who are unhappy in their marriage adopt the belief that when there is trouble in paradise and the marriage goes through turbulent water, then it is time to jump ship.

That is when unhappy people claim they married the wrong person. They say he or she was not my soulmate. They divorce and begin the search for their true soulmate. This is nothing more than an excuse to get out of an unwanted situation. If you are married, the person you are married to is your spiritual mate.

If we would only stay plugged into the Omniscient God, He will lead us to our divine spouse. We must learn to submit to His will and follow His plans not worldly legends. Husband and wife are spiritual mates in that they become one flesh. They are spiritually, physically, and emotionally united to each other. God designed a process for man and woman to join in holy matrimony. In other words, God said, it is not good for man to be alone, so he made a helper suitable for him.

According to scripture, God caused Adam to fall into a deep sleep. While Adam was sleeping, God took one of his ribs and closed up the place with flesh. From that one rib, God made a woman for Adam. She was bone of his bone and flesh of his flesh. She was a different yet complimentary being; a being who was sexually, emotionally, and physically different, yet made from the substance of Adam. Why did God do it this way? I believe it was God's intention for a man to connect spiritually to the woman in holy wedlock.

Mark 10:7-9, declares, "For this reason a man will leave his father and mother and be united to his wife, and the two will become one flesh. So, they are no longer two, but one flesh. Therefore what God has joined together, let no one separate."

True spiritual oneness is only possible when we view it from a biblical perspective.

MADE For God

When I was living in sin, I was a mess. Lust is a temptation and an evil that can consume even the most devout Christian. It is born of Satan and the flesh. Every single one of us is subject to lust. If we are to overcome it, we must let the strength of the Lord be our defense. My decision making was overshadowed by sex. I was so obsessed with sexual thoughts, feelings and behaviors it was affecting my health, job, relationships and other parts of my life. It was so bad, that I risked being late to work to get my fix. On one occasion, I travelled six hours on a highway in Naples, Italy to quench an all-consuming fire. I was so hungry for sex with my boyfriend, that I put my military career in jeopardy. My moral convictions and my lifestyle did not align with the bible. The nexus between promiscuity and sexual sin was strong. Both conditions are regarded as compulsive and pathological qualities, closely related to hyper-sexuality.

Hyper-sexuality is an excessive preoccupation with sexual fantasies, urges or behaviors that is difficult to control. I was not suffering from hyper-sexuality. My actions were not exclusively about lust, sex and sexual satisfaction. My sexual activity was a demonstration of love. Even if I were hypersexual, it was not because I was a nymphomaniac. I only got intense cravings for sex with the man I was dating at the time, because I loved him and wanted him to reciprocate. The problem with this faulty thinking is that when I acted on my sexual urges, I threw caution to the wind and disregarded the red flags. When you mistake lust for love your spiritual eyes and ears become dull. If it was love, why did I feel dirty and impure every time I removed my clothes and got naked before a man I was not married to yet? The reason being, my body was not created to be defiled by premarital sex. I was made for God.

I was stuck in a mud bog. It was a complicated situation and I did not know how to get out of it. Yet, God speaks to us even in our mess. He spoke to me about my unsanctified conduct several times before. All I had to do was listen and follow His leading, but it is not as easy as it sounds. Being young and immature, I did not turn to the bible or prayer for help. I chose not to pay attention to the voice of God. I tuned Him out and persisted in carrying on. I knew there were consequences to sexual sin, yet that did not stop me. Every time I laid with him, I got up from the bed with his spirit; thus, creating a soul tie.

We had been sleeping together for a year when we received the news that the military was transferring him to Norfolk, Virginia, while I was being transferred to Iceland. We both agreed long distance relationships do not stand the test of time. I thought we should break it off and move on. However, he wanted to try the long-distance relationship, I refused. Six months prior to us leaving Italy he proposed; thoughtlessly I said yes.

Sister, when sexual sin is at work within our soul, our perspective concerning ourselves becomes deeply skewed and keeps us from seeing clearly. Our body was not made for sexual immorality, it was made for the Lord. The Lord cares about our bodies *(1 Corinthians 6:12-14)* and wants us to be free from lust. The bible affirms you must cleanse yourself of what is unfit so that you will become a vessel for honor; sanctified and useful to the Master and prepared for every good work. Listen, I wanted to live a holy life and I knew deep down inside I needed to stop, but I lacked self-control.

Lustful desires lead to wrongful choices. Disaster is sure to come when we rush ahead with our own plan and push God's plan aside. Let me be clear here. It is unwise to do this. Trust me when I say, it never turns out well. The best decision you can ever make is to submit your choices to God's plan and be willing to give up an opportunity when you sense God does not want you to move forward with that decision.

Think back to when you were a little girl. You trusted your mother and father to teach you how to make smart decisions. Well, the same is true of God. He is our heavenly Father and with outstretched hands, He will make certain that every decision you make is not regrettable. With His help your decision will produce good and not bad. Even if you make the wrong decision, His grace and mercy shall sustain and strengthen you. His grace will follow you through every season and stage of life. *"He will love you with an everlasting love because He is faithful"* (*Jeremiah 31:2-3*).

Here is some practical advice. When it comes to making decisions, I recommend you make sure you evaluate the choice according to God's written word in light of the way that God has designed you. Err on the side of caution. Not fearful, but cautious. Ask yourself the following questions: Are there risks associated with the decision? Do I have total peace? Is this the right time for this? Will waiting be better? Do I trust God to close the door? Then, wait to hear from God. He is the consultant, the coach, and the counselor. Try as we might, some things just do not work out. However, remember that even our most damaging decisions can be redeemed to honor and glorify Him in due time.

Misinformed By the Culture

Deception distorts biblical truth. It is the root cause of women unseeingly connecting with the wrong man. Engaging with a man who lacks spiritual integrity, typically leads a woman to compromise her values. We find ourselves involved in ungodly activities we have no business in participating. Anytime we overindulge in fleshly desires, it separates us from God. Holiness demands adherence to rules, which guard against immoral conduct. Holiness requires pure worship and wholesome conduct in mind, body and spirit. Holiness cannot be gained if we overlook the warnings found in scripture.

1 Peter 1:15-16 says: "But just as he who called you is holy, so be holy in all you do; for it is written: Be holy, because I am holy."

All parts of our lives and character should be in the process of becoming conformed both inwardly and outwardly, to God's standards. I was born in a culture of comfort, entitlement and self-indulgence. I knew nothing about honoring God with my body. My dear, loving mother was responsible for the design of my mind; helping create a systematic pattern of thoughts followed with action. How I interacted with men and my opinion of them was planted, not just by my mother, but also by television, books and magazines. The thoughts were programmed into me at an early age and were so deeply embedded into my mind that they would automatically direct my decisions without me realizing what I was doing or why I was doing it. I learned to do what I observed my mother and my aunts doing.

Please do not misunderstand what I am affirming. My moral compass was weak, but not completely dismantled. I still had the ability to judge right from wrong and act accordingly; however, I was conditioned. When you are conditioned, you do not learn the behavior naturally; rather you are trained over time to anticipate a particular outcome. Promiscuity was a learned behavior. It was normal and familiar, but I tried to cover it up in an attempt to defend my actions. I was convinced I had a valid reason for what I was doing. Promiscuity was the sinful behavior I learned from my mother who bore me in sin.

Sometimes we sin in ignorance or presumption. The bible says you and I were born into sin. We start life with a strong deadly inclination to sin, which is our sinful nature. Our nature is egocentric or self-centered. We are born desiring our own way, rather than God's will. My mother only passed on to me what she was taught. It was not intentional; she was not trying to teach me to do wrong. It was generational indoctrination. Her mother imparted the behavior to her and she passed it on to me. It became normal and familiar to sleep with a man before he gave me his last name.

We are in a sexual revolution; our mind is constantly being bombarded with sexual innuendos that make it acceptable to fulfill our sexual appetite, however we want. It is like-going to the all you can eat buffet and sampling everything that looks tasty. The devil does his best to convince every woman that God is cheating them out of the best that life has to offer. He has been up to the same schemes for generations; using Hollywood to perpetuate an explicit sexual lifestyle that goes against every moral code in the Bible. He makes the sin so inviting, so thrilling and so exciting as to subtly insist that if you stop having sex with your boyfriend, he will leave you for another girl. It is an illusion, pure trickery. The enemy will whisper in your ear, "If you stop sleeping with him you will miss out on your dream of being his wife, having the perfect home, perfect children, perfect husband, luxury car, and yearly vacations." What the devil will not tell you, is that if you continue doing it your way, your relationship will be built on sinking sand rather than on a firm foundation which is found in the Word and in our relationship with God.

Since the beginning of time, Satan has used sex to create a cultural climate that lures us away from the holiness that God has called in us. Take for instance, the women's movement of the 1960's and 70's. The intent was to dismantle workplace inequality, such as a denial of access to better jobs and salary inequity, via anti-discrimination laws. Since that, time women have been obsessed with money, power and prestige, using their body to get what they want.

I am not minimizing the efforts it took to win the right for women to get an education or voting rights or careers that were meaningful. My argument is that since that time promiscuity and sexual immorality have risen. Every day women are barraged with subliminal messages from television, the internet, magazines, movies, romance novels and music that the key to a woman getting the love and attention she wants is attained by sleeping with a man or men.

Out of fear, poor self-esteem, insecurity, we believe the lie; defending our position knowing we are in the wrong. Yet, convinced we have a valid reason for our actions. The truth is we had no business crossing sexual boundaries prohibited by God. We do not weigh the benefits of that relationship against the cost in terms of how it might affect future relationships. When we engage in emotional affairs, physical intimacy, and mental fantasies about having sex with men other than the man we are married to, we are treading on shaky ground. We jeopardize our sexual integrity and undermine God's plan to grant ultimate sexual and emotional fulfillment with our future husbands. Wait on God. Do not resent his timing and carelessly pursue sexual pleasure without his blessing. Good sex comes to those who wait.

SHACKING Up

The mantra: "Make love not war" originated with the hippies and other student movements. It was a slogan used throughout the 1960's and 1970's to protest and speak out against the Vietnam war, but later became the standard for sexual conduct. During that era, Madonna was singing, "Like a Virgin, yet her lifestyle was not suggestive of a woman who was waiting until marriage to have sex.

When I recall my pre-teen years, I was impulsive. If it felt right, I did it. At the age of sixteen I did whatever felt good at that moment. At the age of eighteen, I enlisted in the United States Navy where I continued to do what felt good. At nineteen, I was pregnant and un-married. At twenty I was married and by age twenty-four I was divorced and a single mother of a four-year-old daughter; struggling to make it from one paycheck to the next. A year later, I was living with the man I was dating. I told myself it was okay. We were in a relationship, I loved him, and he loved me. No more cold, lonely nights. As an added benefit, I could have sex seven days a week if I wanted.

Wake up! The real truth is, shacking up is never a good idea; here is the reason why. The relationship will probably end because any relationship without commitment has a short life span. Take heed to what Solomon said regarding long life.

"And if you walk in obedience to me and keep my decrees and commands as David your father did, I will give you a long life" (1 Kings 3:14). The verse cautions us to avoid letting our own wisdom make us proud, careless or presumptuous.

The consequences of shacking are numerous. To the women who have children, your kids are three times as likely to be expelled from school or to experience early pregnancy. They are five times more likely to live in poverty, and twenty-two times more likely to be incarcerated. Why? Because you chose cohabitation.

Shacking will make couples lazy. Once the dating ends, the relationship changes. Living together removes the, being your best self, part of the relationship. If you are living with a man, waiting on him to pop the big question, all while giving him the benefits of marriage; he can become indolent and be unwilling to take the next step in your relationship.

If the statements above are not convincing enough, then here is a more compelling reason to not shack up. Simply put, a godly woman should not be shacking up with her beau. The bible considers shacking up as the opposite of a legitimate marriage. A genuine marriage consists of a union between a man and a woman who have made a commitment to one another in accordance to God's holy word. Even if you are shacking up part-time; staying at his apartment for the weekend, it is still considered shacking no matter how you dice the onion.

If Jesus was still on earth today, would we dare ask his approval to move in with our boyfriend? I believe Jesus would have said; "Daughter, do not act thoughtlessly, but understand what God wants you to do" *(Ephesian 5:17)*. Sister, you know shacking up with a man would not please the Father, so why would you even ask such a question.

Whenever I think back to that time in my life before the divorce, I cannot help but wonder what made me think the relationship would last. There existed all the benefits of marriage, sex, having a handyman to help around the house, buying groceries together, cooking meals together; but there was no guarantee he would be faithful or loving. It was foolish thinking. I was so blind that I could not see a problem with shacking up. I told myself, "We will be engaged soon, so it is okay", or "I am just getting a feel for what it would be like when we finally get married." These were lies I told myself, because I wanted desperately to be loved. Beloved, God wants us to keep our standards high, act wisely and do well. Living with and/or having sex with a guy that is not your husband overrides the becoming one flesh concept. How so? Because both people have left their separateness to live and be together as a couple, as one. A couple living together is a component firmly reserved for God's original design for marriage. It is not meant to be done outside of this specific God-ordained relationship; for to do so is superseding God's design with one's own personal view and preferences.

"That is why a man leaves his father and mother and is united to his wife, and they become one flesh. Adam and his wife were both naked, and they felt no shame" (Genesis 2:24).

The passage stipulates a man will leave his father and mother and be united to his wife and they will become one flesh without shame. There is no need to address or build a list against the promising problems when a man and woman live together before marriage. The supreme argument against it is that God ordains from the very beginning of humanity's existence that leaving, cleaving, and living together as one is for marriage only. As one flesh, the husband and wife will become family to each other, with all of the legal and relationship rights and privileges that come with being closely connected. To do otherwise, whether knowingly or unknowingly, is a clear defiance of God's design for marriage.

Marriage is an institution blessed by God and considered a sacred bond between a man and woman. Shacking is pursuing one's own course for the present and rejecting God's will. Individual ignorance or willful ignorance does not excuse the violation of God's design. Shacking will always be a violation and it will always fall short of God's righteous and holy standard.

Because sexual sin is an ever-present reality of life, it is essential that we have sufficient self-control with the help of the Holy Spirit. Alternatively, if we are trapped in behavior not pleasing to God, we must fight to be free. This requires consistent, thoughtful study of God's Word and a huge effort to build an awareness of its presence. That is how we break free from being ensnared. If we want to beat sin to the punch, we must first become aware of it. You cannot become aware of sin, if it does not make you uncomfortable. Ignorance must be swapped with godly knowledge and a willingness to have a transformed mind. In whatever context it appears throughout scripture, sin is viewed as failure, as succumbing, not overcoming. Each time we sin, we suffer a defeat in life's overall purpose.

"Do you not know that your bodies are temples of the Holy Spirit, who is in you, whom you have received from God? You are not your own; You were bought at a price. Therefore, honor God with your bodies" (1 Corinthians 6:19-20).

Overcoming sexual sin is a formidable task, but not a hopeless one. One reason why it is not hopeless is that God judges us individually, but with the same righteous standard. According to our natural talents, gifts, dedication, faithfulness, discipline, time sacrificed, and energies exerted to overcome the challenges we face. He knows we are all capable of conquering all categories of sin. It is up to us to believe we can do all things through Jesus Christ who gives us the strength and the will power to do the impossible *(Philippians 4:13).*

The ultimate standard is the holy, righteous character of the Father and Son. Thankfully, we are neither measured against God's performance or His son, nor any other human's performance. We are not in competition against others. God looks at us separately and He simply wants to bring us back into oneness with Him, not merely intellectually, but also in attitude and conduct. Strive for spiritual oneness with God. Oneness with God opens the door of intimacy and understanding. It is a place of peace and contentment. Are you ready to experience spiritual oneness with God?

Pearls of Shattered Dreams

The enemy is a master strategist. He patiently waits for the right time to launch his attack. The Word of God advises us to be alert and clearheaded. *"Be alert and of sober mind. Your enemy the devil prowls around like a roaring lion looking for someone to devour"* (1 Peter 5:8). No other force is set against married couples, nor against impending marriage, as is the devil. He will do whatever he can to sabotage the marriage before you even utter the words, "I do". God created us with a human heart, which has the capacity for passionate desire so that we would long after Him and His righteousness *(Psalm 42:1-2)* and not pursue sexual or materialistic desires.

After desire has been fulfilled, it gives birth to sin and when it is full-grown, gives birth to death. Shortly after I met him, I began sinning. My ex-husband's charisma was so powerful, it was challenging to resist the temptation; even though Jesus said he would give me a way out, but I did not take it. When we first met the chemistry between us was electric. Every time I was with him, my emotions were out of control. He was everything I thought I wanted in a husband. I was sure I had found my soulmate, but after we married, he changed. He was emotionally detached, required constant, excessive admiration, expected to be recognized as superior even without achievements that warrant it. Turns out these were characteristics of a narcissistic person. When you are not following God's guidelines for marriage you will not see a man's true character.

During my period of solitude and self-actualization, God showed me how I agreed to marrying the wrong man. In times of doubt, I followed my own advice. It is imperative for us to give ourselves to God and seek His guidance. *"Trust in the LORD with all your heart and lean not on your own understanding; in all your ways submit to him, and he will make your paths straight" (Proverbs 3:5-6).* The scripture implies that if we decide not to trust the Lord with our whole heart, and we choose to lean on our own understanding, then we will surely go in the wrong direction. The most powerful weapon against sexual impurity is humility. When we humble ourselves and confess our sin, He is just to forgive. Disobedience and lack of close fellowship with God, leads to marrying someone whom He did not desire you to marry. Even in the worst instance of us choosing someone whom we should not have married, God is sovereign and in control. He can turn any situation around so that we still benefit.

Pearls of Hope

Giants represent the problems we face. Thinking I made the right choice in marriage, I never anticipated seeing the divorce giant. Divorce was the giant that threatened my enthusiasm for life. It strived to destroy my health, my happiness and my peace; replacing it with depression and despair. Divorce is so burdensome, it tricks you into thinking there is a colossal giant; that will bring you to ruin aiming to slay your hope for a better tomorrow. God never promised life would be a walk in the park. However, Jesus promised he would be with us every step of the way. That being said, we should not be concerned with the giant; it is how we deal with the giant that determines our survival. You do not win the battle against a bully without a spiritual strategy. It is not by our might or by our own power; it is by the Spirit of God.

A good friend of mine shared a riveting story of her husband's unfaithfulness. She loved her husband deeply, but his betrayal was more than she could bear. She wanted to take their two-year-old son and leave him. What stopped her from leaving was location. They were a military family living on an island in Guam and she did not have the financial resources to fly back to the United States. Furthermore, her husband would have to sign the paperwork to authorize the flight. My friend could not get away from her giant. What does one do in that situation? You stay, and you deal with it. You face the giant. That is exactly what my friend did.

Today, my girlfriend and her husband are celebrating more than twenty-six years of marriage. I believe God positioned her in Guam for a purpose. First of all, she was far away from family members who might have interfered in her process. Mom and dad would have tried to add their two cents and the well-meaning pastor would have counseled them on forgiving one another and reconciling. I believe she was where she needed to be at that precise moment in time for God to teach her how to forgive.

Reflecting on my personal giants of fear and depression after the divorce. I knew the giants of fear and depression had to be defeated, it was the how that had me stuck. After being married for thirteen years; suddenly you find yourself alone and single again. It is tempting to jump immediately into a relationship and risk accepting less than God's best for your life. Like me, you may believe the lie that you will never experience love again with a godly man or you will have to settle for any stray man who comes along.

After my marriage ended, I would have welcomed anything that, walked, talked and looked like a man. Something happened to change all of that when I realized that in every season of life, whether we are celebrating or mourning, wrestling or rejoicing, questioning or trusting, we can hold fast to hope. The Bible says, *"Praise be to the God and Father of our Lord Jesus Christ! In his great mercy he has given us new birth into a living hope through the resurrection of Jesus Christ from the dead" (1 Peter 1:3).*

You see God bound himself with an oath so that those who were given a promise could be perfectly sure that He would never change his mind. Hope deferred makes the heart sick, no one likes waiting. We want what we want, because it feels good to get what we want. However, when our expectations are delayed for a long time, we can experience disillusionment and a loss of hope.

In some cases, prolonged waiting for what we eagerly desire can cause affliction that it begins to cause us to be sick. Deferred means to put off or drag out as in a long drawn out process. Hope deferred can look like many things: a long-term battle with cancer or an agonizing job search or lingering depression from a divorce or unanswered prayer for remarriage/marriage or a heartbreaking string of broken relationships.

As we eagerly hope for God to fulfil something important, the waiting can seem like an eternity. It is as if God is postponing our request, and the longing we feel can make our heart sick. Our heart embodies our mental and emotional core and causes despair and affliction. I was becoming anxious and frustrated with being single year after year. I wanted my prayers to be answered. When our prayers are answered, we are encouraged. The second part of *Proverbs 13:12* tells us *"Hope deferred makes the heart sick, but a longing fulfilled is a tree of life."* The tree of life represents renewal. When we obtain the good thing we desire, we experience a reviving of soul.

Where was my good thing? It was temporarily on hold. My job was to wait patiently and trust Him. God told me He would bring me out from a lifestyle of sexual sin and He did. God said I would remarry, and I will. If God tells you He is going to do it, then you better believe He will. Waiting is an opportunity to trust God and allow Him to work in our heart and strengthen our character. If we look forward to something we do not have yet, we must wait patiently and remain hopeful and confident that He who promised will keep his promise.

Just as a ship's anchor holds firmly to the seabed, your hope is secure and immovable. It is anchored in God. Anchored means, Jesus is our hope and anchor who will keep us in the midst of storms. He is the one who is able to keep us steadfast and unmovable in spite of the tides of life. I prayed: "Dear Lord, I try my best every day to remain optimistic, but sometimes I become pessimistic. Lord, if I lose my hope, please assure me that your plans are better than my dreams." Then, I remembered *Hebrews 6:19, " We have this hope as an anchor for the soul, firm and secure. It enters the inner sanctuary behind the curtain, where our forerunner, Jesus, has entered on our behalf. He has become a high priest forever, in the order of Melchizedek."*

It was an epic battle, but I won the grand prize which is hope. I won because I professed daily that I am anchored in optimism. Jesus Christ grounded me in self-control, perseverance, strength and hope for a better tomorrow. Ask God with honesty, openness and sincerity to help you slay the giant in your life; it does not matter what it is, He will do it. This truth should give you greater hope, confidence, encouragement and assurance. I learned that unfulfilled desires and deferred hope could lead to rich encounters with the Savior.

When hope deferred makes you sick, look to Jesus Christ. *"But now, Lord, what do I look for? My hope is in you (Psalm 39:7).* My hope is built on nothing less than Jesus Christ and I will keep standing on the solid rock of Jesus Christ. Not on the sinking sands of doubt. Not on past hurt and pain. My hope is living and active through Jesus Christ! I am a woman of hope. I am patiently waiting on God to do something outrageously wonderful in my life. I expect God to give me everything I need at the appropriate time. My only hope is in Christ alone, he will not disappoint for he is a *"strong and trustworthy anchor for my soul"* (Hebrews 6:19, NLT).

Pearls of Gratefulness

Thank you, Lord, for my divorce. You read it correctly. I am giving thanks to God for every outrageous circumstance surrounding my divorce. My second divorce was official in 2008. I am a two-time divorcee. There is no shame and no condemnation. In courtroom language, it means I am innocent, not guilty. All accusations are false, and God said: "Berthena, my verdict is not guilty." I am grateful I survived those devastating experiences. What a wonderful God I serve.

As a believer in the resurrected, Jesus Christ, I do not have to worry about being condemned for my actions. *1 John 3:14,* authorizes me to say with boldness and confidence I have passed from death to life. Death was likened to thirteen years of marriage that withered away into nothing. It was like that fig tree that Jesus cursed; because it was not bearing good fruit when it was supposed to, thus it was dead. Life representing new beginnings and renewed joy. I even give thanks for the sorrow and the unbearable pain and shame I experienced when my marriage ended. You probably think I am a little crazy for giving God thanks after the divorce. Is she joking or insane or maybe in denial? Maybe she was not really in love. None of the above. I am not being fake. I am definitely not trying to appear super spiritual either; I am being real.

Listen, insanity, or going crazy is a choice. Intellectually, I wanted to solve my marriage problem before I lost my mind. I wanted to try to make things better because I did not want to go through another life changing, shattering event. I had already been through one divorce and now I was going through another one. My life once again was going to be changed, without my permission. It was not something I welcomed with open arms. I did not enter into a second marriage expecting a breakup. It was brutal, nasty, and very painful. Despite the excessive legal fees, a ruthless, cutthroat custody battle, an indifferent judge, bias in-laws and lying neighbors who only knew one side of the story, I remained grateful. After months of negotiation and mediation, which resulted in two people still unwilling to compromise, the judge granted our divorce. That part was finally over, and I was thankful.

Although I got over that hurdle, it was not over. Then came the late-night tears of defeat and despair, because I felt as if I had lost everything. My days were just as long as my nights. Many days I went to sleep with tears streaming down my face like rain and woke with swollen eyes and concerned looks from the kids. Friends and family members called often; checking in to make sure I was not suicidal. I am thankful for those calls, because many nights I asked God to give me death as a sweet relief from my broken heart.

To make matters worse, multiple storms continued to flood in after the separation. Sometimes back to back with no time to take the next breath. One instance, my ex-husband showed up at our son's games with his new girlfriend; this fueled my anger, causing me to go deeper into depression. To see that he could so easily move on and find another woman to replace me made me feel worthless. Then I began having financial problems, due to the judge's order to pay child support. Then an evil and diabolical Chief Petty Officer at my military command tried to persuade the Command Chaplain to send me on a one-year deployment back to Iraq. Then my teenage daughter; secretly grieving the loss of several friendships began to suffer from emotional stress and anxiety. I could not deal with another crisis. I felt as fragile as brittle paper. One insensitive word about the divorce, one unexpected phone call from a bill collector, or one call from the school with bad news would have caused a nervous breakdown.

Yet I remained close to God. I began to focus on the positive in my life; my children, my military career, my health, loving friends and family. The grace of God covered me like a warm blanket in winter. God was my strong tower when I was hurting so deep within, feeling like I wanted to give up and die. Without God, I would be in a local hospital with a straight jacket; monitored by a group of psychiatric doctors peering through a small, square glass window.

Gratefulness. Nothing can ever compare to the comfort of the Holy Spirit when you are beat down with depression and sadness is hovering over you like a dark cloud. I have experienced His goodness for myself. He made me to be an overcomer and I am grateful. I was struck down, but I am still standing. I am grateful to God for sheltering me under the shadow of His wings and keeping me from ruin.

Pearls of Independence

Research shows there is one divorce happening every thirty-six seconds. That is nearly twenty-four hundred divorces per day, sixteen thousand-eight hundred divorces per week and eight hundred seventy-six thousand divorces a year. Yet, we live in a world that encourages women to be strong and independent without God, but we need God twenty-four hours a day and seven days a week.

Consider the song titled "*Independent Women*" by Beyoncé. Are you familiar with it? The song encourages women to be independent. The urban dictionary describes an independent woman as one who pays her own bills. She is a woman who has a substantial amount of money and she can buy whatever she wants. This woman more than likely thinks that money makes her valuable. That is commendable. It is all right to be able to support yourself. Nothing wrong with that. It only becomes a problem when you are independent without God. Money comes, and it goes but God is constant. If the independent woman loses her job what will she do? What will she do if the extravagant items she accumulated had to be auctioned or her home was in foreclosure? Even if the situation were not that extreme, it can happen to anyone. If you search Google for celebrities who filed bankruptcy, you will find many.

What I do not like about the song is that it depicts a woman who is a loner who thrives on her own independence. She bought the luxury car, the three-story single-family home, red bottom shoes, a diamonds and pearls without the help of a man. According to the song, she is independent. At what cost?

Was it worth being lonely? Selfish? Help-depraved? Money hungry? Emotionally detached? In my experience, material objects and money do not matter when your world is hit by the force similar to a tornado.

The independence Beyoncé is marketing leaves God out of the picture. It does not consider that an independent attitude could be holding a woman back from true love. If you are acting like a man, it is difficult to attract one. Her song gives the impression that strong, ambitious women do not need anyone. A woman taking on the masculine role in her professional career may have helped her gain socio-economic status and recognition, but when it comes to a relationship, too much independence may have an opposite effect. It may push men away.

After divorce a majority of women have to start from ground zero. After my divorce, I was not wealthy, but I had enough money to sustain my two kids and myself. It still took me several years to get my finances back on track. The harsh reality is that after divorce, women experience disproportionate declines in household income and standard of living as well as sharp increases in the risk of poverty. Women may also face a higher risk of losing homeownership. Women's lower chances of remarriage and responsibilities as a single parent may further impede their path to economic recovery.

Sister do not be that woman who dances to the beat of the *"Independent Women"* song, raising your hands to signify your independence and vowing to live life independent of God and man. Promising not to allow another man into your heart, because you were hurt so badly, now you no longer trust men. Do not be the woman who thinks that her bank account will give continuous joy and everlasting peace. Money can buy many things, but it cannot buy genuine love, it does not stop the tears at night and it definitely does not replace the love of God.

Did your independent attitude, along with I can handle it on my own, keep you from an emotional and psychological breakdown? Did your savings and checking account heal your fragmented heart? Were you comforted by all your wealth when you saw your ex-husband at the gas station or the gym or at the grocery store with his new wife or girlfriend?

Regardless of how independent you think you are, stop and remember the faithfulness of a loving God who picked you up from the floor when you were curled up soaking the carpet with your tears. During difficult times, it is wise to call on God for extra strength. His strength will help sustain us when our natural strength fails. Do not ever be ashamed when you feel weak, hopeless, desperate, or alone. Remember what the Bible says in *2 Corinthians 12:10: "That is why, for Christ's sake, I delight in weaknesses, in insults, in hardships, in persecutions, in difficulties. For when I am weak, then I am strong."*

When I was in pain, who helped me? God. I did not have to go it alone. Jesus was not being facetious when He said cast your cares on me for my yoke is easy and my burden is light. He said I could release it, because it was never meant for me to hold. If you have lost the connection because of hurt. Release it and tap back into your femininity. Femininity is more about being. It is about responding, receiving, being joyful, being vulnerable, setting the pace, listening to the Holy Spirit, letting things flow and unfold naturally. It is about trusting and relaxing, while your heart remains open to receiving the love you deserve. It is time we learn to reconcile being strong and independent with the Lord's readiness to guide us to a loving spouse who will care and protect us. Let go and let God handle it. Independent women still need to depend on God.

$\mathscr{Pearls}$ to Protect the Heart

Ladies stop sharing so much with men. Godly women who long to protect their heart and long to be women of sexual integrity must be careful about the words they speak. Our words have power; they can empower, build up, motivate, encourage, commend, bring laughter, joy, and happiness to the people we have contact with. Our words can entice, seduce, lure, tempt, trap, or trick the opposite sex. The bible says the tongue is a restless evil, full of deadly poison. Any words spoken to bless others are respectable. Profanity, and perverted sexual language should never be spoken by a godly woman; that is bizarre and sinful. It is as strange as salt water and fresh water coming out of the same spring together. It is as weird as olive trees growing figs.

There some things-you cannot do with the opposite sex; but so many women are falling into that trap. A wink here, a too tight hug there, or a too long gaze across the sea of heads at church. Nah-uh ladies, antics like this can only end up in sexual sin. Women also use language and body language together to send a loud message that can be perceived as, "she wants to have sex with me". This sort of behavior can lead to sexual sin.

You know how it goes; a woman meets a stranger at a party, then ten minutes after the conversation starts, she is deep into a very personal and very detailed story about how she just caught her husband cheating on her or how she misses the sexual intimacy. It does not seem to matter that she just met the man she is more than happy to reveal the most intimate details of her life. It is a classic case of oversharing.

Such conversations imply that she is sexually available, or emotionally needy.

Often, oversharing is sometimes an unconscious act from women who have recently ended their marriage and were accustomed to the closeness made available through marriage. They do not realize until after the fact that they have just disclosed major details about their personal lives. Sometimes, over sharers are not aware of their behavior until midway through the conversation, when suddenly they find themselves feeling vulnerable for revealing too much info. In other cases, they are aware the entire time that they are oversharing, but do not see it as problematic. It is troubling to me that so many unmarried women are oblivious or do not pay attention to the impact of their words when mingling with the opposite sex. What sexual sin do you know of that did not take place without intimate words being exchanged? Like a fisherman casting the bait, maybe he says things like this to get the woman to compromise:

"I was hoping to see your beautiful smile today."

"Can I give you a ride home, so we can continue our conversation?"

"My wife is on a business trip; I sure could use some company."

"Does your man appreciate how wonderful you are?"

And perhaps she responds with:

"I enjoyed going to lunch with you today, are you free tomorrow?"

"I like the way those jeans look on you."

"You look like you work out, can we work out together?"

"What would your wife say if she knew we were having these conversations?"

His wife would probably have a few choice words for you and him. If you say you belong to God, but do not control your tongue, you are fooling yourself and your religion is worthless *(1 James 1:26)*. Let us face it, women talk too much. We share information about our desires, our goals, our hurt, our victories, our achievements; intimate details about our life. Topics reserved for our spouse. Would you change the way you live if you knew that every word and thought would be examined by God first? David asked God in *Psalm 19:14* to approve his words and his reflections as though they were offerings brought to the altar. When you talk to men, are your words a sweet-smelling incense to God's nostrils?

SAY NO TO UnGodly Passions

Regard lust as a warning sign of danger. When you notice that you are attracted to a person of the opposite sex and preoccupied with thoughts of him or her, your desires may lead you to sin. That is what happened to me. Do not be like the immoral woman who strategized to lure the man. You know exactly what I mean. This type of woman dresses in provocative clothing, revealing skin and body parts like the people you find on the nudist beach in Haulover Beach, Florida. No doubt our world is filled with women who seem to have nothing more in mind than to tempt a man into an illicit relationship. I look at women today, and in my mind, I ask, "Did her mama or grandmama see what she was wearing when she left the house?"

There are women who live a life of seduction. The Bible says, where the seeds of discontent have been sown, the seductress is ready to pounce on her prey. The seductress plays on the felt needs of the man for approval, respect, sexual fulfillment, physical closeness, and fleshly pleasure. She knows how men are wired, and she exploits it to her own advantage and evil purposes. *Proverbs 3:5: "For the lips of the adulterous woman drip honey, and her speech is smoother than oil"*

Proverbs 7:21: "With persuasive words she led him astray; she seduced him with her smooth talk."

Words are the ammunition found in the seductress armory; conversation is used to flatter her prey so that he feels really good about himself. Deceptive language lures him into her trap. The words of a seductress go beyond being complimentary *(see also Proverbs 6:24,7:5)*. As the man's ego grows, so does his sexual appetite. Her verbal persuasions continue by appealing to his imagination; presenting a visual picture of what she wants to do to him, where and how she wants to do it. *(Proverbs 7:14-18)* She is an expert in deception, persuading her prey into believing there will be no consequences or that the consequences are not that terrible *(Proverbs 7:19-20)*. She uses her beauty, her eyes, her body, her clothes, and her words to muddle the man's judgment such that he becomes caught up in the moment *(Proverbs 7:10,13)*. This is why Joseph immediately fled when Potiphar's wife approached him in a seductive manner *(Genesis 39:12)*; he knew she was a seductress and without any hesitation, he ran from her. Otherwise, staying would have ruined his reputation.

In my opinion, the seductress is a lonely, unfulfilled woman. She persuades men with smooth talk, because she has lust in her heart. She sets a trap for the man, because she thinks it is the only way to get a man. She does not care if she is criticized for lacking self-respect. Her ultimate purpose and intent are to please herself by reducing her prey to a loaf of bread. The seductress is not interested in the well-being of the man, though she may well enjoy seeing him be pleased with her. In other words, she is there for her own appetite, to feast upon the precious life of the unsuspecting victim just as Potiphar's wife tried to feast on Joseph *(Genesis 39:6-7)*.

Going back to the Bible, God has condemned any sexual bond outside of marriage, because He knows just how destructive it is to those involved in the act and to those hurt by its betrayal of trust. Those who commit sexual immorality spurn God and His will, and the end is destruction *(Proverbs 7:27)*. There are ways to stop the spirit of seduction. You can take definite steps to avoid sexual sin by guarding your mind. Stop listening to Marvin Gaye's "Sexual Healing", Elvis Presley top ten love songs and the 1970's oldies but goodies. Music can take you on a stroll down memory lane; reminding you of the good ole days.

I have memories of skipping class in high school to meet a cute boy that showed interest. We met in the gym, behind the school bleachers. I consented to his demands for kisses and let him fondle my body. Did I stop him? I most certainly did not. Should I have set boundaries? Yes. My excuse was, "It felt good and all my other friends were doing it." Ladies, we are no longer high school teenagers. When we were children we thought and behaved like children. Now, we are mature women of God capable of controlling our thought life and actions. Real and satisfying sexual intimacy is a natural outflow of emotional and spiritual intimacy rather than a selfish thought process of "it feels good". Sexual immorality will never satisfy, but doing things God's way always will.

Avoid Tempting Settings

Keep away from settings and friends that tempt you to sin. All of us have at least one sister-friend who enjoys having a good time. By a good time, I mean she may think it is okay to meet a guy and sleep with him the same night. Be aware that when you commit to remain celibate until you marry/remarry. There may be some that will try to convince you, that you are being unreasonable trying to be celibate. If a date pressures you, do not compromise. Instead, do not have any further discussions with this person and resolve to date only fellow believers who share your convictions. The Bible is clear about this; maintaining your sexual integrity is not optional. Neither is getting romantically involved with someone who does not share your faith *(2 Corinthians 6:14)*. Above all, God wants to come first in all that you do *(Matthew 6:33)*.

Some people would argue that it is all right to break God's law against sexual sin if nobody gets hurt. In truth, somebody always gets hurt. In the case of adultery, spouses are devastated, and if children are involved, they can be emotionally scarred. Even if the partners escape disease and unwanted pregnancy, they may lose their ability to fulfill commitments, to feel sexual desire, to trust and to be entirely open with another person. God's laws are not arbitrary. They do not forbid good, clean fun; rather they warn us against destroying ourselves through unwise actions or running ahead of God's timetable for remarriage.

Do not think only of the moment; focus on the future. Today's sexual thrill may lead to tomorrows ruin. Recognize the strategies of temptation and learn to run away from them hurriedly. Your life must be so full of God's Word and wisdom that not even if Idris Elba or David Beckman or Tom Cruise asked you out for a date, you would be able to say no without hesitation. Unless they are unmarried, one hundred percent sold out for Jesus and ready for a committed relationship leading to marriage.

Make sure your life reflects righteousness and holiness. The only way to accomplish this is to ask God to help you change your desires so that you resist fleshly desires. Heed the warning in Proverbs, Chapter 7. The chapter was written for men, but it is not just for men. After you have healed from your divorce, seek after your purpose. Women who have a purpose without aim or direction, become empty and unstable. They become vulnerable to temptation.

After experiencing the benefits of marriage such as sexual intimacy, it can be appealing to settle for less than God's best. You may believe the lie that you will never find a godly man, and that you will have to accept whoever comes along. Not so. One way to avoid the temptation of settling is to know what is acceptable and what is not, to both you and God, before you give your heart to another man.

My advice is to stop being in such a rush to date. Moving slow will give you time to understand yourself and the factors that contributed to your divorce. Do yourself a huge favor and slow down before getting into a serious relationship. The men are not going anywhere. Besides, slowing down gives you time to heal, and will allow you to assess the man who wants to court you. In addition, you are more likely to make a godly choice when the right man approaches you, because you would have followed God's timeline and not your own.

SET Boundaries

First, let us discuss flirting, there is no such thing as harmless flirting. All flirting is suggestive to some degree and we are better off without it. Perhaps you find flirting fun and meaningless, but it ceases to be that when you direct it at someone who does not share the same opinion of it as you. There are compliments, and there is flirting. The lines can become blurred rather quickly. Flirting is a dangerous game for Christian women because it reeks of worldly ways. We have no business trying to attract men or be attracted to them with the use of smooth one-liners that have no purpose in the Christian life. Do you want a godly husband? Then you need to be a godly woman who seeks the Lord first, because of your relationship with God the right one for you will see you as a potential wife.

Some women are won over by gifts from a man. Use caution when accepting gifts from men. Refusing a gift from a man is not looking a gift horse in the mouth. What are the man's intentions by giving you that gift? What does he expect in return? I do not care whether the man is Christian or not, if you are not married or at least betrothed to the guy, you have no business accepting his gifts. A box of Godiva chocolate may seem kind and thoughtful at first, but if that man is interested in you and you are not, then you are heading for a difficult time trying to shake him off. Just be upfront with the man and say that you would rather not accept anything from him.

Let us discuss attention seeking. Learn to nip unwanted attention immediately. I understand the allure of having someone interested in you. Most of us enjoy the attention of a man. It is nice to have a man giving us his undivided devotion, and it's very flattering. In the beginning, it makes us feel special until he starts to get too serious; now you do not want to be bothered. If you were not interested in the guy, why on earth did you lead him on? Why even have him wondering if you liked him? Remember, men and women think differently, and we are not mind readers, so you can never comprehend what is going on in the interested guy's mind. It is best to keep it godly and be transparent about your intentions so that there is no room for misinterpretation. There is a very thin line between love and hate; the guy that professed love to you a month ago can seek your destruction if he thinks you led him on.

Here is a big no-no. Discussing your past marital issues with the opposite sex, unless you are courting and moving toward marriage, is dangerous. Like an activist speaking out against social injustice; you are inviting trouble into your life. Just think about it. You have been talking to brother Mark about your ex-husband's shortcomings and he has been taking notes. He begins to fulfill the role that you had hoped your ex-husband would fill, and before you know it, you both succumb to sexual temptation. It is frighteningly easy to give into temptation, especially when you are outside the will of God. Keep your issues between yourself and a trusted spiritual mentor or counselor.

Valentine Day is approaching. Another Valentine's Day spent alone. I know it gets lonely sometimes during cuffing season. Holidays and birthdays are difficult times of the year. However, seeking comfort from the opposite sex, unless it is your biological brother, is never a smart idea. When you are feeling vulnerable, receiving support from a fellow Christian is a natural thing to do. When you actively seek comfort from the opposite sex, this is how scandals start. A Christian woman sought the guidance and comfort of her pastor, spending countless hours in counseling sessions. Their willpower began to weaken, and their flesh took precedence over everything else. Next thing you know, the woman is pregnant with the pastor's baby. Or perhaps a man and woman in the church sought comfort from each other and committed fornication. The list goes on. Take your troubles to the Lord first and then seek out suitable comfort and guidance from a trustworthy female friend.

Would someone please answer these two questions. Why would you want to be unequally yoked with a non-believer? Is there a problem with waiting on God for the right man He has for you? We cannot seek after men who are in the world because they can pull you away from God quicker than you can draw them to God. What we should be attracted to is a man who puts God first in everything, not a handsome face, an athletic body, a rich man, a charming man or even someone who makes you laugh. Look for the godly traits first and you might just find that the man that God sent to you is the perfect fit for you. Keep praying, remain faithful and obedient to God and you will meet the one.

Finally, I know that many women will argue with me concerning this, but let us be honest: kissing, petting, cuddling are all inappropriate when you are not married to the guy. Keep your hands and your lips to yourself until you get married. When you are dating someone, it should be for the purpose of getting married. You are not trying to have a friendship with benefits. We all know that the flesh is weak, right? So, when you are courting a guy and you kiss him, or he kisses you, lust is going to come speeding in faster than you realize. If we say that we are women of God, then we need to start acting like it in word and in deed.

We are not like other women. We are the daughters of a Holy God. We have a standard to uphold before the world. It will destroy our testimony if non-believers saw us French kissing our boyfriend or allowing him to cup our derriere or press up against us in an intimate manner.

Until you are ready for marriage, dedicate yourself to things of the Lord and keep yourself pure. If the guy you are dating tries to make you feel guilty, then he does not fear the Lord. Men and women are to be devoted to one another in love, honoring one another above ourselves (Romans 12:10). The Apostle Paul in Romans 12 verse 10 is describing what it means to live as a self-sacrificing Christian. Our love for each other must be as brothers and sisters in Christ; sincere and genuine. We are to outdo one another in showing honor to each other. If every man and woman acted on this, every person in the body of Christ would always feel deeply honored. All of us would be motivated to check our motives when interacting with the opposite sex. We would be stirred to ask: "How can I show more honor to my brother?"

New Day Ahead

You were a treasure in a fragile clay jar and you fought your way through many trials and tribulations; fighting hard against deception, depression, anger and unforgiveness along the journey. Though you were badly hurt, it did not mean you were entirely hopeless and lost. Nor were you ever without a friend; you were not destroyed. Though you thought you were at the end of your rope, you were never at the end of your hope. God never abandons His own. All the riskiness, pain, and humiliation were opportunities for Jesus Christ to demonstrate his power and presence in and through you. It is time to carry on and fulfill your destiny, looking to God for strength. When opposition threatens to rob you of victory, remember that no one can destroy what God has accomplished through you. God's grace is all you need because His power works best in weakness. This is a new day. God's power dwells within you. Though you were pressed on every side, you grasped the truth that your own human strength was inadequate to bring you through the valley of disillusionment.

God designed our minds to observe our thoughts, catch those that are bad, and get rid of them. An undisciplined mind is filled with a continuous stream of worries, fears and distorted perceptions that trigger processes that cause deterioration in the mind and body. Because your mind is affected by your thoughts, you must take charge of what you think. Stop the negative judgements, thoughts, and feelings before they start. You cannot afford not to bring your thoughts into captivity to Christ Jesus *(2 Corinthians 10:5)*. Make your mind realize that it is your servant, not your master, starting today. You have been set free; believe that you are free and walk in your freedom today.

Today, a new day is dawning. God wants to alter your thinking so that it lines up with what he thinks about you. You are a pearl without ruin. God has prepared divine blessings for you each day. Incorporate daily declarations into your morning and you will disrupt the devil and stop him from conspiring against you to delay or hinder your freedom from sexual sin. Do not abandon declarations and neglect to command your day with God's Word. By your words you decree a thing and God says: *"it shall be established unto thee."* What you establish through the power of your decrees and declarations on earth will be established in heaven. What you confess you possess. What you say is what you get. What you bind on earth will be bound in heaven. Words taken directly from scripture are the only words capable of producing the kind of joyous life you are longing for.

Believe that whatever you say in this season will become a reality in your life. Remember each day brings new blessings and promises God has prepared just for you. Each day there may be a new battle the enemy has prepared for you in an attempt to keep you from claiming abundant life. If you rise up early and command your day to line up with God's Word for your life, then the enemy has no power to frustrate and misdirect your day.

God desires to drop dew upon your life every morning. He wants to open His good treasure to you. To receive new blessings, it is your responsibility to command the heavens to bless your land and the work of your hands, to release you from every struggle, and every temptation. The arm of flesh will fail you, but God will sustain you in every spiritual endeavor. What you declare from your lips shall become a part of your life. Confessing or decreeing a thing is a verbal exercise that brings a response from God. *Job 22:28 (NLT)* declares that *"You will succeed in whatever you choose to do, and light will shine on the road ahead of you."*

Rise early

"Have you ever given orders to the morning, or shown the dawn its place, that it might take the earth by the edges and shake the wicked out of it? (Job 38:12-13).

Throughout the scriptures, God commanded His servants to rise early in the morning and go. You should rise early and command your morning. Command your day from the night before and possess the gate of restoration. Rise early to obtain the promises, the victories, the spoils of war and the blessings of abundance that the Lord has prepared for you. If you have not commanded your morning before you go, you may find that the enemy has been working well in advance of your arrival to block your progress and ruin your life. Be vigilant and consistent!

You must understand as Jesus did, that your day actually begins at night when the sun sets, not when it rises. Before you see the sunrise, much spiritual activity has taken place in the heavens and in the Earth, in preparation for the next day. So, as the sun goes down between the first watch (6:00 pm to 9:00 pm) begin to command your day!

"Now when Daniel learned that the decree had been published, he went home to his upstairs room where the windows opened toward Jerusalem. Three times a day he got down on his knees and prayed, giving thanks to his God, just as he had done before" (Daniel 6:10).

Each day confess every past or recent, conscious or unconscious, known and unknown sin in your heart, thoughts and flesh. Confessions is important so that the accuser will not have room to hinder your prayers. Break the cycle of sexual attraction today. Break cycles of disappointment, unfruitfulness, unfilled expectations, loneliness, and compromise. You can dethrone every form of sin from its place of power when you make confession a daily part of your life. Make sure there is no ill will or evil intent in your heart. Remove all rocks of offense. Seek forgiveness and forgive others immediately. As you pray for God to break every weakness in your life, He will shut the door to every demonic opening to your life.

Prayer will give you the authority to bind negative thoughts and words by speaking God's Word. You will destroy the forces that are at work; prohibiting the answers to your prayers. Pray for divine deliverance from sexual sin and release divine protection for you and your family. Pray for a release of God's Power, the Arm of the Lord, the Fire of God, and Sword of the Lord and the Blood of Jesus to protect your heart. Pray to uncover and destroy every hidden attack or agenda of the enemy. The enemy will try to drag you back to the past, but when you pray and fast you will be able to break free from sexual sin and walk in liberty. I have provided several declarations to help you affirm what God says in His Word.

$\mathscr{P}\textit{earls}$ of Declaration

Blessings and favor be upon you. I am thrilled that you have taken this step in establishing these powerful declarations over your life. As you embark on this journey, may your strength be renewed everyday like a new morning. May God, stir up the wells of purpose inside of you. May your heart be found clean. Let the doors open and favor overtake you. May the wickedness of the adversary be broken at the beginning of a new day. For this is a new season for you to rise up. Behold, let the wells within you spring forth and produce new steams of increase, blessings and greatness in the days ahead. You are blessed, in the mighty Name of Jesus Christ. I seal every declaration in the Blood of the Lamb, Jesus Christ. Amen.

Declarations:

Father, I decree and declare that I will be anxious for nothing. But in everything by prayer and supplication with thanksgiving, I will make my requests known to You. (Philippians 4:6-8)

Lord, I decree and declare that I will awake every morning in faith knowing that You hear and answer my prayer. Because I bring my needs to You, I will walk in the peace of God that surpasses understanding, and it will guard my heart and mind. (Proverbs 4:23)

Lord, I decree and declare that in stillness and quietness I will patiently wait for You, and You will lead me in the way I should go. (Psalm 31:3)

Lord, I decree and declare that all good thing that God has provided for me today will manifest. Bring complete order to my day as I seek You first and make Your will my priority. I rejoice in the new day You have given me. I praise You for making it fruitful and productive. (Philippians 1:6)

Lord, I decree and declare that all that you have determined to establish in my life for your glory will not be postponed. You have determined that I will flourish in every work and prosper in everything you have called me to do. (Jeremiah 31:28)

Lord, I decree and declare that I will no longer walk around under a banner of shame. Because of the shed Blood of Jesus Christ, I am free and without shame. (Hebrews 12:2)

Lord, I decree and declare this is the start of a new day. I have been given this day to use it .for good and not waste it. (Lamentations 3:23 & Isaiah 60:1)

About The Author

Berthena Jackson is the mother of two adult children, and the grandmother of two beautiful grandchildren. She is an Intercessor who has a heart to see women of every ethnicity set free and walking in all that Jesus has purchased for them as they carry Christ into their world each day, awakened to His nature and who they are in Him. Her desire is to encourage women to seek a deeper relationship with the Lord and see them walk in the fullness of their identity and inheritance in Christ. Having overcome obstacles and bondages in her own life, she shares her life experiences to encourage women to believe that no weapon fashioned against them will prosper. With God all things are possible.

For speaking engagements and/or more information:
berthenajackson@gmail.com